Laws of Wealth Study Manual

Billy Epperhart

Copyright 2025–Billy Epperhart

All rights reserved. This book is protected by the copyright laws of the United States of America. This book may not be copied or reprinted for commercial gain or profit. The use of short quotations or occasional page copying for personal or group study is permitted and encouraged. Permission will be granted upon request. Unless otherwise indicated, all scripture quotations are taken from the *King James Version* of the Bible. Used by permission. All rights reserved.

All emphasis within Scripture quotations is the author's own. Please note that Harrison House's publishing style capitalizes certain pronouns in Scripture that refer to the Father, Son, and Holy Spirit, and may differ from some publishers' styles. Take note that the name satan and related names are not capitalized. We choose not to acknowledge him, even to the point of violating grammatical rules.

Harrison House P.O. Box 310, Shippensburg, PA 17257-0310

This book and all other Harrison House's books are available at Christian bookstores and distributors worldwide.

Reach us on the Internet: www.harrisonhouse.com.

ISBN 13 TP: 978-1-6675-1259-4

ISBN 13 eBook: 978-1-6675-1260-0

Contents

1. What Is Kingdom Wealth? — 1
2. The #1 Threat to Kingdom Wealth — 9
3. The Triple X Factor — 17
4. The Law of Change — 25
5. The Law of Wisdom — 33
6. The Law of Stewardship — 41
7. The Law of Lift — 49
8. The Law of Income — 57
9. The Law of Conversion — 65
10. The Law of Diligence — 73
11. The Law of Risk — 81
12. The Law of Leverage and Acceleration — 89
13. The Law of Compounding — 97
14. The Law of Philanthrovesting — 105
15. The Law of Transformation — 113
16. The Law of the Triple Bottom Line — 119

About the Author — 125
About the Publisher — 127

Chapter 1

What Is Kingdom Wealth?

"But seek first the kingdom of God and His righteousness, and all these things shall be added to you." (Matthew 6:33, NKJV)

I remember the day I reached financial freedom like it was yesterday. I was sitting in my car, drinking a quad-shot americano, when one of my property managers called me. He said, "Billy, you did it. You can quit your job." Years of planning, investing, and praying had finally come to fruition. I had built enough passive income from real estate to replace my salary. It should've been a mountaintop moment—and in many ways, it was. But behind the joy, there was an unsettling feeling. A twinge of guilt. Could I, a pastor, genuinely celebrate financial success in the marketplace? Was it wrong to care about wealth?

At the time, it was frowned upon to be bi-vocational or to pursue business as a pastor. The assumption was that if you trusted God, He'd provide—and that meant steering clear of entrepreneurial ambition. But I couldn't shake the feeling that my love for business, finance, and investing was more than a carnal distraction. I began to wrestle with the bigger picture: what if this part of me—the business-minded part—was also created by God, for God?

This journey led me into a deeper revelation of the Kingdom of God. One conversation changed everything. A friend pointed me to Matthew 6:33, a verse I'd read many times before. But for the first time, I saw it differently. I had always interpreted it as "seek Jesus first" or "put God first," but it says *seek first the kingdom of God*. That distinction radically transformed how I saw my calling, my career, and my wealth. Seeking the Kingdom meant seeking God's rule on earth, His values, His priorities, His purpose in every realm of life—including finances.

So let me ask you a question: What if your wealth isn't about you? What if your earnings, your career, your investments, your inheritance—what if all of it is designed to serve something greater? To fund revival. To rebuild cities. To transform nations. That's Kingdom wealth. Are you ready to embrace it?

Focus Point

"But seek first the kingdom of God and His righteousness, and all these things shall be added to you." (Matthew 6:33, NKJV)

This verse is the cornerstone of Kingdom wealth. It reorients our understanding of provision—placing God's Kingdom not just as a spiritual ideal, but as the very framework through which our lives, our finances, and our influence find meaning. Seeking first the Kingdom doesn't mean excluding finances—it means including them in God's divine plan.

Main Theme

This chapter sets the foundation for everything that follows in the *Laws of Wealth*. It challenges the reader to move from a limited "Gospel of Salvation" mindset into the expansive "Gospel of the Kingdom." Kingdom wealth is not merely about having money—it is about understanding that everything we possess can be a tool for God's redemptive work on earth. This chapter introduces us to the concept of *Ekklesia*—the Church not as an isolated institution, but as a people deployed into every sphere of influence to bring about transformation. By defining Kingdom wealth as a partnership with God to fulfill His purposes, this chapter lays the groundwork for a life of abundance, stewardship, and impact.

> **"Kingdom wealth is not about getting more, but about giving more—to God, to people, and to the world He's called you to transform."**

Key Scriptures

- *"But seek first the kingdom of God and His righteousness, and all these things shall be added to you."* (Matthew 6:33, NKJV)

- *"And I will give you the keys of the kingdom of heaven, and whatever you bind on earth will be bound in heaven, and whatever you loose on earth will be loosed in heaven."* (Matthew 16:19, NKJV)
- *"For he raised us from the dead along with Christ and seated us with him in the heavenly realms because we are united with Christ Jesus."* (Ephesians 2:6, NLT)

Key Points

- **The Kingdom Is Now** The Kingdom of God is not just for the afterlife. Jesus said it is *at hand*. Kingdom wealth acknowledges the present reality of God's rule and reign.
- **You Are an Ambassador** As believers, we are seated with Christ and called to carry His authority. This includes our influence in finances and the marketplace.
- **The Church Is Ekklesia** Jesus didn't call us to build religious monuments. He called us to infiltrate and transform every area of society with Kingdom values.
- **Marketplace Matters** Business and investing are not "less spiritual." They are mission fields. Wealth built God's way brings His will to earth.
- **Wealth Requires Purpose** Wealth without Kingdom purpose leads to greed. Wealth with Kingdom purpose leads to legacy. You are called to the latter.
- **You're Called to Influence Mountains** Every believer is meant to influence at least two of the seven mountains of culture—family, government, education, business, religion, media, or arts.
- **Money Is Just a Tool** Wealth isn't the end goal. It's a resource to carry out God's vision for reformation and restoration in the earth.

Journaling Questions

This chapter invites you to explore what it really means to pursue Kingdom wealth. Journaling through these themes helps identify where your current beliefs may align more with tradition or fear than with God's truth. As you write, allow the Holy Spirit to show you how your financial life can become a part of God's greater narrative. Reflect on what parts of your thinking need to shift so your money becomes a tool of purpose rather than pressure.

. . .

As you engage with these journaling questions, you may uncover limiting beliefs, misplaced guilt, or untapped passion. You'll begin to sense the Holy Spirit reshaping how you see money—not as a master, but as a servant. This reflection will give you clarity, conviction, and a Kingdom-centered vision for your financial journey ahead.

Redefining Wealth

In what ways have I separated my spiritual life from my financial life? How can I begin to unify them under the Lordship of Jesus?

_____
_____
_____
_____
_____
_____
_____
_____

Ekklesia in Action

How am I currently bringing the Kingdom into my workplace, relationships, and financial decisions?

_____
_____
_____
_____
_____
_____
_____

Marketplace Ministry

Do I believe business can be a calling from God? How has that belief (or lack of it) influenced my decisions?

_____
_____
_____
_____
_____
_____

Mountains of Influence

Which cultural mountains do I feel drawn to? How might God be calling me to influence them?

_____
_____
_____
_____
_____
_____

Tikkun Olam—Repairing the World

If I had unlimited resources, who or what would I invest in to bring God's transformation to the earth?

_____
_____
_____
_____
_____
_____

Actionable Steps

Cultivate a Kingdom Vision
Set aside time this week to write a one-page financial mission statement rooted in Kingdom principles. Define what wealth means for you and how it can serve others.

Equip Your Mind
Choose a book, course, or mentor in Kingdom finance or entrepreneurship. Begin developing a new mindset around money, calling, and impact.

Engage Your Culture
Ask God where He's calling you to bring Kingdom influence—in your job, community, or a mountain of culture. Take one bold step this month to activate that calling.

Personal Reflection

Sometimes, the reason we haven't stepped fully into God's financial purpose for our lives isn't a lack of opportunity—it's a limited vision. As you sit with the truths of this chapter, take a moment to ask yourself: Do I believe God cares about my money? Do I believe He has a plan for it? Invite the Holy Spirit to expand your capacity to dream, plan, and invest with a Kingdom focus.

Let this be a moment of surrender and empowerment. You are not a bystander in the economy of heaven—you are a steward, a builder, and a co-laborer with Christ. Embrace the responsibility, the privilege, and the adventure of building Kingdom wealth with boldness and integrity.

What does Kingdom wealth look like in my life? Where is God asking me to break tradition and step into purpose? And am I willing to use my wealth to impact eternity?

_____
_____
_____
_____
_____
_____
_____

Closing Prayer: *Lord Jesus, thank You for inviting me into the greater story of Your Kingdom. I surrender my ideas of wealth and ask for Your vision instead. Help me steward every dollar, every opportunity, and every moment for Your glory. Teach me to invest in people, purpose, and eternity. Expand my heart, enlarge my vision, and align my finances with Heaven. In Your name, Amen.*

Chapter 2

The #1 Threat to Kingdom Wealth

"No one can serve two masters; for either he will hate the one and love the other, or else he will be loyal to the one and despise the other. You cannot serve God and mammon." (Matthew 6:24, NKJV)

The moment money began flowing into my life at a new level, something unexpected happened. I wasn't just excited—I was anxious. Even fearful. And more than that, I felt a strange grip around my heart that I couldn't immediately define. It was the spirit of mammon. I had pursued wealth for years, but now that it was coming in, I felt its pressure and pull. It wasn't just about money anymore—it was about control. What if I lost it? What if I misused it? What if I relied on it instead of God? I didn't realize it then, but I had crossed a line where money began to challenge my devotion to God.

This isn't a new battle. In fact, Jesus warned about this very thing. Mammon is not simply money; it is a spirit that seeks to replace God as the source of security, identity, and direction. And here's the truth: you don't have to be wealthy to struggle with mammon. Some of the most financially burdened people in the world are under its influence. Because mammon is not about how much you have—it's about who you trust.

God's Word makes it clear: the love of money is a root of all kinds of evil. The issue isn't the presence of wealth—it's the posture of your heart. When you seek first the Kingdom, wealth is a tool. But when you serve mammon, wealth becomes a trap. This chapter exposes how mammon manifests not only in greed, but in fear, hoarding, and insecurity. It shows us the deep biblical foundation for why God must remain our source—even in seasons of abundance.

So let me challenge you with this: Have you unknowingly made mammon your master? Have you held back generosity because of fear? Have you allowed worry to dominate your financial decisions? If so, you're not alone—but you are being called higher. Let this chapter be the moment you draw a line in the sand and reclaim your freedom.

Focus Point

"No one can serve two masters... You cannot serve God and mammon." (Matthew 6:24, NKJV)

This verse unveils the spiritual battle behind wealth. Jesus wasn't simply offering advice—He was drawing a hard boundary. Mammon represents any form of trust or allegiance that challenges God's authority in our hearts. To serve God fully, we must dethrone mammon completely. This is not just about rejecting greed; it's about choosing loyalty.

Main Theme

The #1 threat to Kingdom wealth is not a lack of opportunity, information, or resources—it's allegiance to mammon. Mammon is the counterfeit master that tempts us to rely on money instead of God. This chapter guides readers to recognize mammon's influence and teaches them how to break free through remembrance, worship, and generosity. Drawing from the story of Israel in the wilderness and the Canaanite culture of Baal and Asheroth, it highlights how ancient idolatry still lives today—just with different names. In God's economy, remembrance births gratitude, and gratitude destroys greed. Only when our hearts are rooted in trust and worship can wealth be used for its Kingdom purpose.

"If money becomes your master, you will never walk in the freedom God intended—but if money becomes your servant, the Kingdom will flourish through your hands."

Key Scriptures

- *"For the love of money is a root of all kinds of evil, for which some have strayed from the faith in their greediness, and pierced themselves through with many sorrows."* (1 Timothy 6:10, NKJV)

- *"But remember the Lord your God, for it is he who gives you the ability to produce wealth."* (Deuteronomy 8:18, NIV)
- *"You cannot serve God and mammon."* (Matthew 6:24, NKJV)

KEY POINTS

- **Mammon Is a Spirit, Not Just Money** The spirit of mammon operates wherever trust in money replaces trust in God. This deception can affect the rich or the poor.
- **Worry Reveals Allegiance** Jesus connected mammon with anxiety over provision. Worry is a red flag that you may be trusting money more than your Father.
- **Old Testament Idolatry Still Lives Today** Baal and Asheroth were worshiped for fertility and prosperity—just like today's idols of wealth, status, and security.
- **God Gives the Power to Get Wealth** Provision isn't passive. The ability to create wealth is a God-given partnership, not a divine handout.
- **Remembrance Slays Mammon** Throughout Scripture, God calls His people to remember what He has done. Gratitude makes greed powerless.
- **Generosity Breaks the Spirit of Mammon** Giving confronts mammon head-on. It dethrones selfishness and proves that God—not money—is your source.
- **Mammon Can't Survive in a Heart Full of Worship** A worshiping heart sees money as a tool, not a treasure. Where there is worship, there is no room for worry.

JOURNALING QUESTIONS

This chapter confronts one of the most subtle but destructive spiritual threats to your financial life. Journaling through its truths is crucial to identify where mammon may be influencing your decisions. Whether it shows up as greed, fear, comparison, or worry, writing down your patterns helps you break their power. As you process God's Word through self-reflection, you'll discover new layers of freedom and authority.

Through honest journaling, you'll begin to see how trust, not money, is the true currency of the Kingdom. You may recall situations where fear overtook faith—or where the spirit of mammon led to controlling behavior. These reflections are not to condemn but to correct. The Holy Spirit will guide you into truth, freedom, and a renewed posture of stewardship.

Recognizing Mammon's Grip

What emotions or behaviors reveal that mammon may be influencing me—fear, control, comparison, or reluctance to give?

_____
_____
_____
_____
_____
_____
_____

Worship or Worry?

Do I spend more time in financial anxiety or in worshipful trust toward God as my provider?

_____
_____
_____
_____
_____
_____

Looking Back to Remember

How has God faithfully provided for me in the past? What are three specific testimonies of provision I can recall and thank Him for?

_____
_____
_____
_____

Giving as Warfare

Have I ever experienced breakthrough after a generous act of giving? What did that moment teach me about God's economy?

_____
_____
_____
_____
_____
_____

Rooting My Identity

Do I see myself as a steward or an owner of my resources? How does this affect the way I spend, save, and give?

_____
_____
_____
_____
_____
_____

Actionable Steps

Cultivate Daily Gratitude
Start a gratitude journal focused only on financial blessings, no matter how small. Each day, write one way God provided.

Equip Your Heart for Generosity
Set a giving goal that stretches your faith. Don't wait to "have enough." Begin now by giving strategically and sacrificially.

Engage Your Memory with God's Faithfulness
Create a "Remembrance Wall" in your home or office where you post physical reminders of God's financial provision. Let it inspire worship and silence worry.

Personal Reflection

Where is your trust today? That's the question this chapter asks, not to condemn but to awaken. God's invitation to build Kingdom wealth is holy—but it requires undivided loyalty. As you reflect on your current posture toward money, ask the Holy Spirit to reveal anything that subtly competes with Him in your heart. The goal isn't just to avoid the traps of greed—it's to live fully free, joyfully generous, and deeply rooted in trust.

Surrender is not a loss—it's an exchange. When you lay down the idol of mammon, you pick up the peace of God. It's not about having less; it's about needing less because your confidence is in Him. As you begin to think differently, spend differently, and give differently, you'll discover what it really means to be free.

Am I building my wealth on worship or worry? Where has mammon hidden in my thinking? And what bold step can I take today to reclaim God's rightful place as my provider?

Closing Prayer: *Lord, I repent for every way I have trusted money more than I've trusted You. I break agreement with the spirit of mammon and declare that You alone are my Source. Thank You for the power to create wealth—and for the reminder that I am not a slave to it. Teach me to remember Your faithfulness, to walk in worship, and to give with joy. I trust You fully and follow You boldly. In Jesus' name, Amen.*

Chapter 3

The Triple X Factor

"See, I have set the land before you; go in and possess the land which the Lord swore to your fathers —to Abraham, Isaac, and Jacob—to give to them and their descendants after them."
(Deuteronomy 1:8, NKJV)

I still remember the moment the urgency of financial preparedness gripped me. I had just wrapped up a major conference at my church—a truly powerful event with seven private jets parked outside and some of the most influential leaders in the Kingdom present. Afterward, I headed into the Colorado mountains with a couple of those leaders to rest and recharge. We stood together in a hot springs pool, surrounded by snowcapped beauty, when one of them abruptly turned to me and asked, "Billy, what kind of plans have you made for retirement?" I was caught off guard, but before I could even formulate a response, he dropped a bombshell: "If I didn't have my ministry, I'd be broke in 90 days."

That moment lit a fire under me. This was a man I deeply respected, someone who had "made it" in ministry, yet behind the platform was a terrifying financial vulnerability. I realized then that it wasn't enough to have spiritual purpose—I needed financial stability to carry that purpose forward. I came home from that retreat with a new resolve: to build enough passive income to replace my entire salary and benefits. And I did.

But on that journey, I discovered a big problem: there were a million strategies to make a million dollars, but very few gave a complete picture of how wealth is built—from foundation to fruit, from paycheck to legacy. That's why I developed what I call the *Triple X Factor*. It's the clearest, most comprehensive blueprint I've found for building wealth God's way. Not just wealth for your survival—but wealth for Kingdom transformation.

So I ask you: Do you know where you are in your financial journey? Are you stuck living month to month with no clear path forward? Or are you ready to trade fragmented tips for a holistic plan? The Triple X Factor will not only show you where you are—but where you can go when you partner with God to master your money.

Focus Point

"See, I have set the land before you; go in and possess the land..." (Deuteronomy 1:8, NKJV)

This verse captures the essence of the Triple X Factor. God has already provided the land—opportunity, calling, wealth potential. But He doesn't force it upon us. We must go in, step by step, and possess it. Wealth is not dropped in our laps. It is built intentionally. The Triple X Factor is your map into the land of financial freedom and Kingdom impact.

Main Theme

The Triple X Factor is a clear, strategic framework to help you go from financial survival to supernatural significance. It isn't just about saving or investing—it's about moving from dependence on a job, to passive income, to Kingdom legacy. Each "X" represents a crossing point: First X—when your income surpasses your expenses; Second X—when your passive income replaces your job income; and Third X—when your wealth surpasses your needs and funds your calling. The power of this framework is that it gives language, vision, and practical steps for anyone, at any stage, to build wealth with purpose.

> **"Financial freedom is not the destination—it's the launching pad for Kingdom transformation."**

Key Scriptures

- *"You shall remember the Lord your God, for it is He who gives you power to get wealth."* (Deuteronomy 8:18, NKJV)
- *"Write the vision and make it plain on tablets, that he may run who reads it."* (Habakkuk 2:2, NKJV)

- *"A good man leaves an inheritance to his children's children."* (Proverbs 13:22, NKJV)

Key Points

- **You Need a Complete Framework** Most teachings offer pieces of wealth-building. The Triple X Factor gives you the full journey—from paycheck to purpose.
- **First X: Income Must Exceed Expenses** The journey begins when you take control of your spending. Budgeting, discipline, and margin create the first breakthrough.
- **Second X: Passive Income Replaces Job Income** Freedom happens when your money works for you. You are no longer trading time for money, but stewarding income-producing assets.
- **Third X: Wealth Becomes Kingdom Impact** The goal is not just comfort but calling. Once your needs are met, every dollar can go to advancing the Gospel and transforming lives.
- **Three Levels of Money** Level 1: You work for money. Level 2: Money works for you.
- Level 3: Money works without you. Each level requires new thinking and new strategy.
- **Every Dollar Has a Direction** Tracking your expenses and income with monthly precision empowers you to grow. Vision without numbers is just a dream.
- **You Can Start Now** You don't need a massive portfolio to begin. Start with what you have, chart your income and expenses, and build your first X.

Journaling Questions

This chapter is deeply practical and transformational. Journaling here gives you clarity—not just about your dreams, but about your current reality. When you write your monthly income and expenses, you face truth. When you plot your gaps and progress, you build discipline. And when you imagine reaching your Third X, your heart comes alive with divine purpose. This is more than financial planning—it's vision planning.

. . .

You'll discover where you are and what's next. You may confront areas where spending needs to be curbed or where investing needs to begin. You'll gain clarity, not just in numbers, but in purpose. As you write, expect the Holy Spirit to speak strategy, correction, and hope into your journey.

Starting Where I Am

What are my current monthly expenses and income? Have I taken time to truly calculate the numbers, or am I guessing?

_____
_____
_____
_____
_____

Defining My First X

What needs to change in my financial habits for my income to consistently exceed my expenses?

_____
_____
_____
_____

Vision for Passive Income

What assets or ideas can I begin pursuing to generate income that doesn't require constant time and effort?

_____
_____
_____
_____

Impacting Beyond Myself

If my needs were completely met by passive income, how would I use my excess to serve God's Kingdom?

_____
_____
_____
_____
_____
_____

Building My Chart

Have I created a visual map of my financial growth? How would tracking my progress monthly motivate or challenge me?

_____
_____
_____
_____
_____
_____

Actionable Steps

Cultivate Monthly Awareness
Choose a day each month to log your income and expenses. Plot them on your own Triple X chart and review your progress with prayer and intention.

Equip Yourself with Asset Knowledge
Commit to learning about one new income-producing asset this month—real estate, digital products, small business, or investments. Take a course, read a book, or interview a mentor.

Engage a Bigger Vision

Pray about your Kingdom legacy. Ask God, "What kind of impact do You want me to make with my money?" Then write it down and post it where you'll see it every day.

Personal Reflection

God never intended for you to stay at the base of the mountain. He has invited you into a land of abundance—not just so you can live well, but so you can give well. The Triple X Factor is not about chasing money—it's about chasing vision, with money in its rightful place as your servant, not your master. As you reflect on this chapter, take a moment to ask God where you are and where He's calling you next.

Remember, freedom is not just about debt elimination—it's about destiny fulfillment. There's a harvest waiting, but it requires seed, strategy, and stewardship. Your chart may begin with humble numbers, but if you stay faithful, the outcome will far exceed your expectations.

Where am I on the Triple X chart today? What small action can I take to move toward the next X? And am I willing to let God use my financial journey to fund His eternal mission?

_____
_____
_____
_____
_____
_____
_____
_____
_____
_____
_____
_____
_____
_____
_____
_____
_____
_____

Closing Prayer: *Father, thank You for the blueprint You've given me to steward wealth Your way. Help me embrace vision, discipline, and faith as I walk this journey. Let my income, investments, and influence be aligned with Your Kingdom. I trust You to supply the seed, the wisdom, and the growth. May my finances reflect Your heart, and may my life overflow with generosity and purpose. In Jesus' name, Amen.*

Chapter 4

The Law of Change

"Therefore, if anyone is in Christ, he is a new creation; old things have passed away; behold, all things have become new." (2 Corinthians 5:17, NKJV)

Change doesn't always come softly. Sometimes, it shows up at the kitchen table. I remember the day I held a personal funeral for one of my favorite meals—rice and cream gravy with ketchup. That Southern dish had been a comfort food for years. The combination of melted grease, flour, and whole milk poured over white rice and slathered with Heinz ketchup might sound outrageous to some, but it was home for me. However, as I got older and started making changes for my health, I knew I had to let it go. So I walked into the kitchen, took out my portable communion kit, and said a prayer over the dish: "In Jesus' name, rice and gravy is dead to me." I buried it right there—figuratively, of course. It was a funny moment, but deeply symbolic. That day, I made a decision to change.

Change, even when it's for the better, usually involves loss. You have to let go of something familiar to take hold of something greater. Whether that's a habit, mindset, or way of doing life, change can feel uncomfortable—even painful. But it's essential for growth. And when it comes to building Kingdom wealth, change is non-negotiable. You cannot prosper God's way while clinging to old thinking.

Scripture tells us that following Jesus means becoming a new creation. That means change isn't just an occasional occurrence—it's a way of life. Jesus modeled it, initiated it, and expects it of those who follow Him. From water turning into wine to hearts turning from sin, Jesus disrupted comfort zones at every turn. If we're going to build wealth for the Kingdom, we must adopt a mindset that welcomes transformation.

So here's the question: Are you ready to give God a new wineskin? Because He's ready to pour out new wine. But He won't waste it on an unyielding vessel. The Law of Change demands that we stretch, let go, and grow into the kind of people who can carry the blessings He's eager to release.

Focus Point

"Therefore, if anyone is in Christ, he is a new creation..." (2 Corinthians 5:17, NKJV)

This verse is a bold declaration of divine transformation. Being "in Christ" is not just about salvation—it's about continual change. We don't follow Jesus and stay the same. The old must pass away. The new must rise up. And if we want new financial fruit, we must allow Him to plant new seeds—starting with our mindset.

Main Theme

The Law of Change is the foundational principle that growth requires movement. You can't gain and retain something new while doing things the old way. To build Kingdom wealth, you must be willing to evolve—spiritually, mentally, and practically. Drawing from examples in physics, Scripture, and personal transformation, this chapter shows that real change begins with surrender. It requires rejecting stagnation and embracing new thought patterns. If we want new results, we need new wineskins—hearts, minds, and habits ready for fresh outpouring.

> **"God's blessings are never the issue. The question is, can your mindset hold what He's ready to release?"**

Key Scriptures

- *"No one puts new wine into old wineskins... New wine is put into new wineskins, and both are preserved."* (Matthew 9:17, NKJV)
- *"Then the Lord said... 'You have dwelt long enough at this mountain.'"* (Deuteronomy 1:6, NKJV)

- *"The weapons of our warfare are not carnal... bringing every thought into captivity to the obedience of Christ."* (2 Corinthians 10:4–5, NKJV)

Key Points

- **Change Is the Starting Point of Growth** Nothing new will last if the old remains. Financial increase always begins with personal transformation.
- **Jesus Modeled Radical Change** From miracles to messages, Jesus consistently challenged the status quo. He never left things as they were.
- **New Wine Requires New Wineskins** You can't contain God's fresh revelation with old thinking. Flexibility, not familiarity, attracts the supernatural.
- **Strongholds Are Built Thought by Thought** Negative patterns around money often come from deeply held, unseen beliefs. These must be identified and broken.
- **The Holy Spirit Leads into Change, Not Comfort** Many Christians avoid God's will because it feels unfamiliar. But discomfort isn't always a warning—it's often an invitation.
- **Mindset Determines Capacity** Like the man with the 10-inch skillet, if your internal capacity is small, even large blessings will be thrown back.
- **Transformation Is Intentional, Not Accidental** Change requires decisions, sacrifices, and strategy. You grow your mindset on purpose, not by accident.

Journaling Questions

This chapter calls for personal honesty and courage. Journaling through the Law of Change will help you uncover limiting beliefs, old comfort zones, and areas where your wineskin needs renewal. As you reflect, write not only what needs to change, but what you're willing to let go of. Your words will become your roadmap to breakthrough.

Expect God to expose old ways of thinking that no longer serve you. You'll likely see where you've avoided risk or resisted new paths. This is where freedom begins—by acknowledging what must change and inviting the Holy Spirit to lead the renovation. Your new level of wealth begins with a new level of thought.

Letting Go of the Familiar

What habits, beliefs, or comfort zones am I clinging to that are keeping me from moving forward?

_____
_____
_____
_____
_____
_____
_____

Identifying My Strongholds

What thoughts around money, purpose, or success have I accepted that don't align with God's truth?

_____
_____
_____
_____
_____
_____

Making Room for the New

Where do I sense God calling me to stretch in this season? What am I resisting, and why?

_____
_____
_____
_____
_____
_____

Mindset Inventory

Am I operating with a consumer or a producer mindset? How does that affect my financial decisions?

_____
_____
_____
_____
_____
_____

Expanding My Capacity

What would a "bigger skillet" look like for me? In what area do I need to increase my capacity to receive?

_____
_____
_____
_____
_____
_____

Actionable Steps

Cultivate a New Wineskin
Choose one habit or belief you know is holding you back financially. Replace it with a new, God-aligned action or thought pattern, and practice it for 30 days.

Equip Your Mind with Truth
Find a Scripture that directly counters your biggest financial fear or stronghold. Memorize and declare it daily.

Engage a Change Catalyst
Make a change that stretches you—whether it's giving sacrificially, starting a new venture, or saying no to a comfortable job that no longer fits your calling.

Personal Reflection

Change will always cost you—but not changing will cost you far more. You cannot stay the same and step into the future God has for you. The Kingdom life is a life of movement, and you are called to grow into someone who can carry the weight of blessing and influence. As you reflect, ask God where He wants to stretch you. Let Him show you what to bury and what to build.

He is not trying to take something from you—He's making space for something greater. But He won't pour new wine into an old vessel. Let Him transform your container, so He can overflow your content.

What mindset is God asking me to release? What new thought must I embrace? And am I ready to stretch into the person who can carry more for His Kingdom?

_____
_____
_____
_____
_____
_____
_____
_____
_____
_____
_____
_____
_____
_____
_____
_____
_____

Closing Prayer: *Father, I give You permission to change me. Renew my mind, break every limiting belief, and stretch my capacity. Make me a new wineskin—flexible, teachable, and expectant. I surrender the familiar so I can receive the fullness. Let every stronghold fall, and let Your truth reshape my thoughts and habits. I trust You with the process, and I choose to grow. In Jesus' name, Amen.*

Chapter 5

The Law of Wisdom

"Wisdom is the principal thing; therefore get wisdom. And in all your getting, get understanding." (Proverbs 4:7, NKJV)

There's something special about being a grandfather. I've had the joy of watching all four of my grandsons play baseball, and I love investing in their development. One of my favorite gifts was a full batting cage setup in the backyard, complete with an Iron Mike pitching machine. That machine throws balls with a consistent rhythm—just like in real games—so my grandsons could learn timing, focus, and technique. But as much as that setup helped, there was still no comparison to the real thing. Practice taught them the mechanics. But it wasn't until they got in the game that they learned the deeper lessons—how to react, adapt, and think under pressure.

That's the difference between knowledge and wisdom. Knowledge is knowing *about* something. Wisdom is knowing how to *apply* it. There are a lot of people with information about finances, investments, and success, but they've never stepped into the arena. Wisdom only grows through experience. You can learn in the classroom or the boardroom, but you'll be tested in real life. You don't become wise by watching—you become wise by doing.

This principle holds true in every area of life, but especially in wealth-building. You can read all the books and listen to all the podcasts, but until you take action—invest, fail, learn, adapt—you won't possess true wisdom. This chapter is your call to leave the bleachers and step onto the field. God wants you to be wise stewards, not just informed ones.

So I'll ask: Are you practicing or playing? Are you stuck in preparation, or are you ready to apply what you know with courage and faith? The Law of Wisdom demands action. And wisdom rewards those who engage.

Focus Point

"Wisdom is the principal thing; therefore get wisdom..." (Proverbs 4:7, NKJV)

Solomon, the wisest man to ever live, didn't say to get wealth, fame, or even knowledge first—he said to get wisdom. Because wisdom builds everything else. If you want to build something that lasts—whether a business, a legacy, or a Kingdom impact—it must be built on wisdom. And wisdom is found not just in principles, but in practice.

Main Theme

The Law of Wisdom teaches that you cannot prosper God's way without developing the spiritual and practical insight to manage resources well. It emphasizes that wisdom is more than information—it is tested, applied, and often born through failure. Drawing from biblical truths, sports metaphors, and life experience, this chapter equips readers to move from passive learning to active stewardship. It also clarifies that wisdom isn't reserved for the elite or educated—it is for anyone willing to listen, learn, and act on godly truth.

"Wisdom is knowledge in motion. Until you apply it, it's not working for you—it's just waiting on you."

Key Scriptures

- *"Through wisdom a house is built, and by understanding it is established."* (Proverbs 24:3, NKJV)
- *"If any of you lacks wisdom, let him ask of God, who gives to all liberally... and it will be given to him."* (James 1:5, NKJV)
- *"A wise man will hear and increase learning, and a man of understanding will attain wise counsel."* (Proverbs 1:5, NKJV)

Key Points

- **Wisdom Comes Through Experience** You don't gain wisdom by watching others succeed—you gain it by stepping out, making mistakes, and adjusting your strategy.
- **You Must Get in the Game** Preparation is good, but hesitation can mask as fear. At some point, you must move from studying to starting.
- **Wisdom Multiplies What You Have** It's not about how much you have—it's about how wisely you manage it. Wisdom takes little and turns it into much.
- **God Is the Source of True Wisdom** James 1:5 reminds us that anyone who lacks wisdom can ask—and God will give it generously. You're never alone in decision-making.
- **Wisdom Builds Endurance** Like in baseball, not every swing is a hit. But wisdom teaches you how to stay in the game, adjust your form, and keep going.
- **Discipline Is a Fruit of Wisdom** Wisdom teaches you when to say no, when to wait, and when to act. It shapes your habits as much as your decisions.
- **Wise People Seek Counsel** You don't have to know it all. Wisdom is often found through mentors, advisors, and godly counsel.

Journaling Questions

This chapter offers the opportunity to reflect on your relationship with wisdom. Are you merely collecting information, or are you applying truth? Journaling will help you identify the moments where fear has kept you in analysis paralysis, and the ways God might be prompting you to step forward. It will also challenge you to evaluate how well you seek and apply counsel in your financial journey.

As you write, expect the Holy Spirit to bring clarity. You'll begin to see how your habits, conversations, and decisions reflect your current level of wisdom—and where it's time to grow. Don't be surprised if God also highlights areas where you've been waiting too long to act. Wisdom always leads to obedience.

From Knowledge to Wisdom

What financial or business knowledge have I gathered but not yet applied?

_____
_____
_____
_____
_____
_____
_____

Stepping onto the Field

What is one decision I've been delaying that I know I need to act on? What's been holding me back?

_____
_____
_____
_____
_____
_____

Seeking Counsel

Who in my life carries wisdom in finances or leadership? Have I humbly and intentionally sought their input?

_____
_____
_____
_____
_____
_____

Learning from Mistakes

What lesson has a past financial failure taught me? How can I use that lesson to grow?

_____
_____
_____
_____
_____
_____

God's Wisdom for My Season

What specific area do I need to ask God for wisdom in right now? Have I brought it to Him in prayer?

_____
_____
_____
_____
_____
_____

Actionable Steps

Cultivate a Habit of Application
Choose one piece of financial advice or principle you've heard recently, and apply it within the next seven days. Don't wait—act.

Equip Through Counsel
Schedule a conversation with someone wiser than you financially. Ask good questions and take notes. Apply at least one thing they suggest.

Engage God's Voice Daily

Each morning this week, pray James 1:5 aloud and ask God for specific wisdom for your financial steps. Write down what you sense.

Personal Reflection

Wisdom is not far from you. It's not reserved for the wealthy, the seasoned, or the scholarly—it's available for every believer who's willing to ask, act, and learn. As you reflect on this chapter, invite God to show you where you've delayed action in the name of preparation. He's not looking for perfection—He's looking for participation.

Don't stay stuck in practice mode. Step into the field. Miss a few swings. Adjust your stance. And keep going. That's where wisdom is formed—in motion, in action, and in surrender. You have what you need to begin. God will meet you along the way.

Where have I substituted learning for doing? What decision is God waiting on me to act on? And how can I start walking in wisdom today?

_____
_____
_____
_____
_____
_____
_____
_____
_____
_____
_____
_____
_____
_____
_____
_____
_____
_____

Closing Prayer: *Lord, I thank You that wisdom is available to me. I ask for it now—liberally, generously, and specifically. Help me to apply what I've learned, not just accumulate more knowledge. Show me where to move, whom to ask, and how to obey. Let wisdom guide my finances, my decisions, and my future. I trust You to walk with me through every lesson. In Jesus' name, Amen.*

Chapter 6

The Law of Stewardship

"Moreover it is required in stewards that one be found faithful." (1 Corinthians 4:2, NKJV)

I'll never forget the early days of managing the little I had. Long before investment properties and business ventures, I had to make small but strategic decisions that revealed whether I could be trusted with more. I remember watching how even the smallest financial choices—paying bills on time, giving consistently, budgeting carefully—seemed to determine the momentum of my future. It was in these moments that I began to see a spiritual principle emerge: God doesn't multiply what you mismanage.

That realization shifted everything. I stopped asking for more and started asking, "Am I being faithful with what I already have?" It's easy to pray for increase, but the gateway to increase is stewardship. And stewardship isn't about wealth—it's about faithfulness. How you manage $100 often says more than how you dream about managing $1 million.

Stewardship is the bridge between wisdom and wealth. It's where vision meets responsibility. In the Kingdom of God, ownership is never the goal—faithful management is. This chapter unpacks what it means to be a steward in God's economy, how stewardship is measured, and why it unlocks promotion in both the natural and spiritual realms.

So here's your invitation: Stop asking only for more. Start managing what you have as if it were already multiplied. Because how you treat what's in your hand determines what God puts in your future.

Focus Point

"Moreover it is required in stewards that one be found faithful." (1 Corinthians 4:2, NKJV)

God doesn't require perfection in stewardship—He requires faithfulness. Being a steward means recognizing that nothing you have is yours. Every dollar, every opportunity, every asset belongs to Him. And faithfulness means managing it with diligence, integrity, and vision. Faithful stewardship always precedes Kingdom promotion.

Main Theme

The Law of Stewardship teaches that you are not the owner—you are the manager. In God's Kingdom, increase flows through trust, and trust is built through stewardship. This chapter highlights the difference between ownership and stewardship and explains why God promotes those who manage well, not just those who ask well. With practical wisdom and biblical foundation, it challenges you to evaluate how you manage what you currently possess—time, money, relationships, and opportunities. Because what you do with what you have reveals whether you're ready for what's next.

> **"God won't give you what you're praying for if you're mismanaging what you're already holding."**

Key Scriptures

- *"The earth is the Lord's, and all its fullness, the world and those who dwell therein."* (Psalm 24:1, NKJV)
- *"His lord said to him, 'Well done, good and faithful servant; you were faithful over a few things, I will make you ruler over many things.'"* (Matthew 25:21, NKJV)
- *"If you have not been faithful in what is another man's, who will give you what is your own?"* (Luke 16:12, NKJV)

Key Points

- **Stewardship Begins with Ownership Recognition** Everything belongs to God. When you realize you're not the owner, you start making decisions that honor the true Master.
- **Faithfulness with Little Leads to Increase** God promotes stewards who manage small things well. If you want more, prove faithful where you are.
- **Time, Talent, and Treasure Are All Stewardship Categories** We often focus on money, but God watches how we steward our time, gifts, and influence just as closely.
- **Your Mindset Determines Your Stewardship** A scarcity mindset hoards. A stewardship mindset multiplies. How you think determines how you manage.
- **God Measures Stewardship, Not Success** Success is not just about results—it's about responsibility. God rewards those who manage well, not just those who achieve much.
- **Stewardship Is a Test** Every opportunity you have is an open-book test. How you handle your current season prepares you for your next one.
- **Good Stewardship Protects Legacy** It's not just about you. Faithful management lays a foundation for future generations and Kingdom impact.

Journaling Questions

Stewardship exposes what you truly believe about God, money, and your calling. Journaling through this chapter allows you to evaluate your management style, identify weaknesses, and celebrate where you've been faithful. It's an opportunity to repent for waste and renew your commitment to excellence.

Through reflection, you'll begin to see where small decisions are blocking big breakthroughs. You'll uncover excuses that need to be confronted and habits that need to be shifted. Most of all, you'll recognize areas where God is calling you to step up—not just for your sake, but for the generations after you.

Who Owns What I Have?

Do I truly see God as the owner of my money, resources, and opportunities? What areas am I still treating like they're mine?

_____
_____
_____
_____
_____
_____

My Stewardship Scorecard

How faithfully am I managing my current income, time, and talents? Where am I excelling—and where am I neglecting responsibility?

_____
_____
_____
_____
_____
_____

The Promotion I'm Praying For

Is there something I'm asking God for that I haven't prepared to manage? What needs to change in my current stewardship?

_____
_____
_____
_____
_____
_____

Small Decisions, Big Results

What small financial or lifestyle habits are affecting my long-term fruitfulness?

_____
_____
_____
_____
_____
_____

Legacy-Minded Management

How am I building a foundation for those who come after me? What systems, habits, or investments will outlast me?

_____
_____
_____
_____
_____
_____

Actionable Steps

Cultivate a Daily Ownership Reminder
Each morning this week, declare aloud: "Everything I have belongs to God. I am a faithful steward of what He has entrusted to me."

Equip with Financial Systems
If you don't already have a working monthly budget, create one this week. Use a simple spreadsheet or app to track income and expenses.

Engage a Stewardship Reset
Identify one area—finances, time, talent—where you've been neglectful. Create a 30-day plan to manage it with renewed excellence and accountability.

Personal Reflection

Stewardship is more than a concept—it's a lifestyle. It challenges your pride, sharpens your habits, and reveals your trust. When you stop asking, "What do I want to do with my money?" and start asking, "God, what do You want me to do with *Your* money?"—everything shifts.

Your increase is connected to your integrity. Your promotion is tied to your performance—not in striving, but in faithful responsibility. God wants to trust you with more, but He needs to see faithfulness in the few. That's the proving ground for abundance.

What is God asking me to manage better? What's at stake if I ignore this call? And what could happen if I truly embraced the role of a Kingdom steward?

Closing Prayer: *Father, thank You for entrusting me with resources, opportunities, and influence. I repent for the times I've mismanaged what You've given. Today, I recommit to being a faithful steward—not out of fear, but out of love and reverence. Help me manage with excellence, wisdom, and purpose. Let every decision honor You and prepare me for the next level. In Jesus' name, Amen.*

Chapter 7

The Law of Lift

"But those who wait on the Lord shall renew their strength; they shall mount up with wings like eagles, they shall run and not be weary, they shall walk and not faint." (Isaiah 40:31, NKJV)

I remember a conversation I had while flying on a small plane with a pilot friend of mine. As we soared through the sky, I began asking questions about what makes flight possible. He explained the four fundamental forces of flight: lift, thrust, weight, and drag. Lift is what pulls the plane upward, while weight pulls it downward. Thrust moves it forward, while drag resists that motion. He said, "Billy, if the law of lift is greater than the law of gravity, the plane rises." That struck me. It wasn't that gravity disappeared—it was just that a higher law overrode it.

That principle echoed deep in my spirit. It's the same with life. We are all subject to laws like gravity—the pull of poverty, fear, doubt, and generational patterns. But there's a higher law at work in the Kingdom. The Law of Lift. It doesn't ignore gravity, but it supersedes it. When applied, it enables you to rise above limitations, fears, and even your own past.

The Law of Lift teaches that through applied force—faith, obedience, wisdom, and discipline—you can rise above what once held you down. But this law doesn't activate passively. Just like an airplane needs speed, momentum, and wing structure to generate lift, so too must you align your life with Kingdom dynamics if you want to elevate.

Are you living bound by gravity or propelled by lift? Are you allowing the resistance of life to keep you grounded, or are you building the spiritual systems that allow you to soar? The Law of Lift says: you *can* rise—but only if you're willing to apply the right principles.

Focus Point

"But those who wait on the Lord shall renew their strength; they shall mount up with wings like eagles..." (Isaiah 40:31, NKJV)

This verse is a promise of supernatural elevation. Waiting on God doesn't mean passivity—it means positioning. Those who trust in the Lord and align with His ways receive divine empowerment. Like eagles, they are lifted not by their own striving, but by the unseen wind of God's Spirit. That's the Law of Lift at work.

Main Theme

The Law of Lift teaches that spiritual and financial success doesn't come by avoiding resistance—it comes by learning how to rise through it. This chapter illustrates how principles from physics mirror biblical truth: applying the right forces in the right way enables you to overcome the pull of limitations. It's not about denying gravity (challenges, poverty, fear), but about applying a higher force (faith, obedience, wisdom) that causes you to rise above them. Just as a plane must be built for lift, your life must be structured to carry elevation.

> **"You don't break the law of gravity. You override it with a stronger law—the Law of Lift."**

Key Scriptures

- *"For the law of the Spirit of life in Christ Jesus has made me free from the law of sin and death."* (Romans 8:2, NKJV)
- *"They shall mount up with wings like eagles..."* (Isaiah 40:31, NKJV)
- *"I can do all things through Christ who strengthens me."* (Philippians 4:13, NKJV)

Key Points

- **Lift Requires Structure and Motion** Planes are designed to rise, but they need motion and correct angle to activate lift. Your life must be structured with discipline and momentum to rise.

- **Gravity Still Exists—but It Doesn't Have to Dominate** Challenges will always be present. The question is: have you activated the higher law that enables you to rise above them?
- **Faith and Obedience Generate Spiritual Lift** Just like thrust and lift work together, your faith and obedience must be active and aligned to generate Kingdom elevation.
- **Lift Happens Through Resistance** Planes rise because of air resistance—not in spite of it. Likewise, pressure in your life can help you rise, if you engage it with the right mindset.
- **Your Design Determines Your Altitude** Not every plane is built to fly at the same height. Your spiritual design—your mindset, discipline, and alignment—sets your potential ceiling.
- **Momentum Is Essential** Just as a plane cannot lift without runway speed, your consistency and movement are vital. Stagnation stalls lift.
- **Waiting on the Lord Is an Active Posture** Isaiah 40:31 isn't passive—it's preparational. Waiting means calibrating, aligning, and trusting. It positions you for divine acceleration.

Journaling Questions

This chapter invites you to examine what's keeping you grounded. Journaling through the Law of Lift will expose where resistance is being misinterpreted as failure, and where structural adjustments in your life are needed. It will help you identify what "lift systems" God is calling you to build—habits, disciplines, relationships—that empower you to rise.

As you reflect, you'll start to see how your design may be limiting your altitude. You'll find encouragement that the very resistance you've been avoiding is part of your elevation. And you'll gain clarity on what principles you must begin to activate in order to override the pull of gravity in your spiritual and financial life.

What's Holding Me Down?

What areas of my life currently feel like gravity—pulling me down or keeping me stuck?

_____
_____
_____
_____
_____
_____
_____

Have I Built for Lift?

Do I have the disciplines, habits, and mindset structures in place to support spiritual and financial elevation?

_____
_____
_____
_____
_____
_____

Am I Using Resistance Wisely?

What current challenge could actually be a source of lift if I changed my perspective?

_____
_____
_____
_____
_____
_____
_____

Faith and Obedience Check-In

Am I consistently applying faith and obedience to my financial journey—or am I waiting passively?

_____
_____
_____
_____
_____
_____

My Altitude Assignment

What level of "altitude" is God calling me to in this season? What systems do I need to adjust to get there?

_____
_____
_____
_____
_____
_____

Actionable Steps

Cultivate Spiritual Structure
Choose one spiritual or practical habit (prayer, tithing, planning) that you will commit to daily for the next 21 days to support your internal structure for lift.

Equip with Kingdom Momentum
Write out a simple 30-day plan toward a specific goal—financial, spiritual, or relational—and begin it immediately. Movement fuels lift.

Engage Resistance as Training
Identify one challenge you're currently facing. Write down three ways that resistance could strengthen your faith, skill, or mindset—and use it intentionally.

Personal Reflection

The Law of Lift is one of the most empowering principles in the Kingdom. It teaches you that you are not bound by the limitations of this world. Yes, you will face resistance. Yes, gravity exists. But you have access to a higher law. One that says: "Rise." As you reflect, ask God what systems and structures in your life are ready for refinement so that you can soar.

There's no breakthrough without movement. And no rising without tension. But God has built you for flight. He has placed within you everything necessary to override fear, lack, and defeat. Your job is to align, engage, and move forward—into lift.

What principle do I need to activate to overcome resistance? What new structure must I build to rise? And am I ready to soar at the altitude God has designed for me?

_____
_____
_____
_____
_____
_____
_____
_____
_____
_____
_____
_____
_____
_____
_____
_____
_____
_____
_____
_____

Closing Prayer: *Father, thank You that in Christ I am not bound by fear, limitation, or defeat. Thank You for the Law of Lift—the divine principle that allows me to rise above every weight. Show me where I need to restructure, where I need to move, and where I need to trust. Teach me to engage resistance with faith, and let me soar on the wings of Your strength. In Jesus' name, Amen.*

Chapter 8

The Law of Income

"You shall remember the Lord your God, for it is He who gives you power to get wealth, that He may establish His covenant which He swore to your fathers, as it is this day." (Deuteronomy 8:18, NKJV)

I once heard a man say, "Money isn't everything, but it ranks right up there with oxygen." That might make you laugh, but there's a truth behind the humor. Income is not just about dollars—it's about options. When I first stepped into the journey of increasing income, it wasn't because I wanted luxury—it was because I wanted freedom. I wanted to have the time and flexibility to serve God, bless others, and make Kingdom impact without being shackled by financial limitations.

Most people think income is just about getting paid more for their time. That's a dangerous mindset. If all your income depends on your time, you'll never be free. One of the most powerful shifts I made was learning to separate time from income. When your income is tied solely to hours worked, you've limited your earning capacity—and your influence. I had to learn that income should serve my purpose, not dictate my pace.

The Law of Income teaches that wealth isn't just about saving or giving—it's about producing. It's about building streams of income that flow even when you're not actively working. God gives us the power to get wealth—but that power is unlocked through wisdom, creativity, and intentional stewardship. We're not called to chase money. We're called to build income-producing assets that fund the vision God has placed within us.

So let me ask you: Are you working *for* your income, or is your income starting to work *for* you? It's time to evaluate how you think about money—and start thinking like a producer, not just a consumer or laborer.

Focus Point

"You shall remember the Lord your God, for it is He who gives you power to get wealth..." (Deuteronomy 8:18, NKJV)

This verse reframes the pursuit of income from a self-driven hustle to a God-given mandate. God doesn't just bless—He empowers. He gives you the ability, insight, and opportunity to produce income so that His covenant purposes can be fulfilled through you. Income is not for indulgence; it's for impact.

Main Theme

The Law of Income establishes that your financial future is not based on luck, inheritance, or job promotions—it is based on your ability to produce value. Income is created, not merely received. God empowers believers to generate income through creativity, strategy, and stewardship, not just hourly labor. This chapter exposes the limitations of time-based income and urges readers to begin building income-producing assets. By aligning your mindset with God's design, you begin to unlock sustainable financial growth and Kingdom effectiveness.

> **"Don't just make a living—create a life that generates income aligned with your calling."**

Key Scriptures

- *"A good man leaves an inheritance to his children's children, but the wealth of the sinner is stored up for the righteous."* (Proverbs 13:22, NKJV)
- *"The hand of the diligent makes rich."* (Proverbs 10:4, NKJV)
- *"He who gathers in summer is a wise son; he who sleeps in harvest is a son who causes shame."* (Proverbs 10:5, NKJV)

Key Points

- **Income Reflects Value Creation** You are paid for the value you bring to the marketplace, not just the time you spend. Increase your value, and you'll increase your income.
- **God Empowers Wealth Creation** Wealth doesn't just happen. God gives the power to get wealth, and that power must be activated with diligence, strategy, and purpose.
- **Time-Based Income Limits Freedom** If all your income depends on your physical presence, you've created a ceiling. Passive income breaks that ceiling and multiplies your options.
- **You Must Think Like a Producer** Stop thinking like a worker and start thinking like an owner. Producers build systems and assets that generate revenue long after the work is done.
- **Multiple Streams Bring Stability** Relying on one income stream is risky. Wisdom calls for diversification—real estate, business, investments—guided by prayer and sound counsel.
- **Your Income Serves God's Purpose** Income is not just about lifestyle—it's about legacy and Kingdom impact. More income means more capacity to fund what God wants to do through you.
- **Stewardship Precedes Multiplication** Before God increases your income, He checks your stewardship. Faithful management of your current income opens the door to more.

Journaling Questions

This chapter offers a chance to radically rethink your approach to income. Through journaling, you'll examine where your income currently comes from, how dependent it is on your time, and where God may be calling you to step into new ventures. It will also challenge you to consider how your income can be used for Kingdom purposes beyond just personal comfort.

You'll gain insight into your current earning model and whether it aligns with God's call on your life. You'll also begin to see possibilities for diversification, innovation, and productivity that can free your time and increase your impact. The process will reveal where mindsets need to shift and where new actions must begin.

My Income Story

How have I typically earned income, and what beliefs have shaped that approach?

_____
_____
_____
_____
_____
_____

Income vs. Time

Is my income still fully dependent on my time and effort? What steps can I take to start breaking that pattern?

_____
_____
_____
_____
_____

Producer Mindset

Where am I currently thinking like a worker instead of a producer? What needs to shift?

_____
_____
_____
_____
_____

Kingdom Impact

If my income increased significantly, how would I use it to serve God's purposes and bless others?

_____
_____
_____
_____
_____
_____

God's Wealth Empowerment

Do I truly believe God wants to empower me to create wealth? What would change if I fully believed this?

_____
_____
_____
_____
_____
_____

Actionable Steps

Cultivate Value and Creativity
Write down five ways you could increase your income by creating or offering more value—through skills, services, or products. Choose one and begin researching or acting on it this week.

Equip with Financial Education
Choose one area—real estate, stocks, digital products, side business—and commit to learning about it for the next 30 days. Knowledge is the seed of income innovation.

Engage a Passive Income Strategy

Pray and journal about one area where God may be leading you to build a new stream of income. Take one small step—make a call, start a plan, ask for help—within the next 7 days.

Personal Reflection

Your income isn't just a number—it's a mirror. It reflects your beliefs, your habits, and your sense of purpose. If you want to change the number, you must first change the story. As you reflect on this chapter, ask the Lord to show you where you've accepted limits, where you've avoided responsibility, and where you've underestimated the power He placed within you.

God is not intimidated by big numbers. He's not surprised by your dreams. He *gave* you the ability to produce income, not to hoard it, but to use it to bless, build, and break generational bondage. Income is a tool. And God is calling you to sharpen it.

Am I managing income or building it? Am I working only for today, or creating a financial future that reflects God's vision for my life? And what step must I take today to begin walking in the power to get wealth?

_____
_____
_____
_____
_____
_____
_____
_____
_____
_____
_____
_____
_____
_____
_____
_____
_____

Closing Prayer: *Lord, thank You for giving me the power to get wealth—not for selfish gain, but for Kingdom purpose. Help me see income through Your eyes—not as a burden or idol, but as a tool for transformation. Give me creativity, courage, and clarity as I build streams of income that honor You. I trust You as my Source and ask You to lead me into all You've prepared. In Jesus' name, Amen.*

Chapter 9

The Law of Conversion

"The plans of the diligent lead surely to plenty, but those of everyone who is hasty, surely to poverty." (Proverbs 21:5, NKJV)

In the early days of my journey toward financial transformation, I learned a powerful truth: making money is only part of the equation. One of my most eye-opening moments came when I realized that even if I increased my income, it would amount to very little unless I learned to convert that income into something that worked for me. I had to stop thinking only like a laborer and start thinking like a transformer. Conversion, I discovered, is the secret sauce between income and wealth.

So many people earn income—and lose it just as quickly. Why? Because income that is not intentionally converted into assets, investments, or enterprise is like water poured into a sieve. It may feel good in the moment, but it doesn't last. I had to train myself to think about every dollar not in terms of what I could spend, but in terms of what I could *convert*. Conversion turns money into momentum.

The Law of Conversion is about multiplication. Jesus taught us this when He spoke of the servants who were given talents. The one who multiplied what he was given was rewarded. The one who buried it was rebuked. In the Kingdom, faithfulness is proven not by how much you consume, but by how much you convert. Conversion is not just about finances—it's a mindset that sees every resource as seed.

So let me ask you: Are you converting your income into lasting impact? Or are you consuming what should be working for you? The Law of Conversion holds the key to moving from survival to stewardship—and from stewardship to surplus.

Focus Point

"The plans of the diligent lead surely to plenty..." (Proverbs 21:5, NKJV)

This verse doesn't say that hustle or desperation lead to plenty—it says *diligent planning* does. Conversion requires discipline and a strategy. Wealth is not a result of luck; it's the outcome of a lifestyle of intentional transformation. When you make a plan to convert your income into assets or value, you begin walking the path to plenty.

Main Theme

The Law of Conversion teaches that income is not the end goal—transformation is. The difference between those who stay stuck financially and those who build wealth often lies in what they do *after* they receive money. This chapter unpacks how intentional conversion—of income into assets, of ideas into enterprises, and of moments into momentum—creates long-term fruitfulness. Without conversion, income dries up. With conversion, resources multiply. Kingdom wealth is built not by accumulation but by transformation.

"You don't get wealthy by earning—you get wealthy by converting."

Key Scriptures

- *"Then he who had received the five talents went and traded with them, and made another five talents."* (Matthew 25:16, NKJV)
- *"There is desirable treasure, and oil in the dwelling of the wise, but a foolish man squanders it."* (Proverbs 21:20, NKJV)
- *"Through wisdom a house is built, and by understanding it is established; by knowledge the rooms are filled with all precious and pleasant riches."* (Proverbs 24:3–4, NKJV)

Key Points

- **Conversion Requires Vision Beyond the Moment** You must train yourself to see every dollar, idea, and opportunity not just as provision—but as a seed with potential.
- **Income Must Be Transformed to Create Wealth** Earning is not the same as building. If income isn't converted into assets, it disappears without lasting fruit.
- **Money Is a Tool, Not a Trophy** Wealth builders don't admire their income—they assign it. Every dollar should be given an assignment that leads to multiplication.
- **Diligence + Planning = Conversion Power** The process of converting income demands intentional plans and daily discipline. You can't convert what you don't control.
- **Waste Is the Enemy of Wealth** In the absence of a plan, money gets spent. Conversion requires that you manage your finances with purpose, not emotion.
- **Conversion Honors God's Trust in You** Just like the faithful servants in the parable, those who multiply what they are given show that they are worthy of more.
- **Assets Work While You Rest** Conversion turns money into workers—investments, systems, and assets that produce even when you're not actively laboring.

Journaling Questions

This chapter is a wake-up call to stop passive spending and start intentional building. Journaling through the Law of Conversion will challenge you to examine your financial behavior, assess what you've built, and create a vision for future multiplication. It is an invitation to partner

As you journal, you'll identify where you've been consuming rather than converting. You'll gain insight into the kinds of investments or systems you should be building. And most importantly, you'll renew your commitment to being a faithful steward who multiplies, not just maintains, what God has entrusted to you.

How Am I Using What I've Been Given?

Am I multiplying or merely maintaining the income and resources God has entrusted to me?

_____
_____
_____
_____
_____
_____
_____
_____

My Money Assignment

Do I assign every dollar a job that leads to growth, or do I let money slip away unaccounted for?

_____
_____
_____
_____
_____
_____
_____
_____

The Asset Audit

What am I currently building or owning that works for me, even when I'm not working?

_____
_____
_____
_____
_____
_____

Consumer vs. Converter

Have I developed the mindset of a converter, or am I still operating as a consumer?

_____
_____
_____
_____
_____
_____

The Long View

What am I doing now that will continue bearing fruit five years from today?

_____
_____
_____
_____
_____
_____

Actionable Steps

Cultivate a Conversion Mindset
For the next 7 days, every time you receive or spend money, ask: "Is this building something?" Write down what could be converted instead of consumed.

Equip with a Financial Flow Strategy
Create a visual flowchart of your current income and spending. Then, add a new plan showing how you can begin redirecting at least 10% into assets or investments.

Engage a Conversion Habit
Choose one area of financial life—budgeting, investing, saving—and take one concrete step this week to convert income into a multiplying asset.

Personal Reflection

The Law of Conversion isn't just about money. It's about honoring what God has placed in your hand. Every resource He entrusts to you is an invitation to transform, multiply, and steward with vision. As you reflect on this chapter, remember: the difference between survival and surplus is not what you earn—it's what you *do* with what you earn.

It's time to stop spending like a consumer and start building like a steward. You have the mind of Christ. You have access to the wisdom of God. And you have the power to convert income into lasting, fruitful, and eternal impact.

Am I spending money or converting it? Am I building something that will outlast me? And what small shift can I make today that will change my financial future forever?

Closing Prayer: *Father, thank You for entrusting me with resources, ideas, and income. Forgive me for where I've consumed rather than converted. Teach me to see what's in my hand not just as provision, but as seed for multiplication. Give me wisdom, strategy, and courage to build something that brings You glory and blesses generations to come. In Jesus' name, Amen.*

CHAPTER 10

THE LAW OF DILIGENCE

"The soul of a lazy man desires, and has nothing; but the soul of the diligent shall be made rich."
(Proverbs 13:4, NKJV)

When I was young and just beginning to understand the path of financial freedom, I used to believe that passion and prayer were enough. I had vision. I had purpose. But it wasn't until I embraced diligence that things started to shift. I remember a season when I was working a full-time job, building a side business, and studying everything I could about money and stewardship. It wasn't glamorous, but it was fruitful. And through that season of daily, intentional effort, I saw breakthrough begin to emerge—not overnight, but over time.

Diligence isn't about working endlessly. It's about working intentionally and consistently toward your God-given goals. So many people confuse busyness with diligence. They think spinning their wheels means they're making progress. But diligence is more than motion—it's focused productivity that compounds over time. Proverbs tells us that the diligent will rule, while the lazy become subject to others. This is a law not just of life, but of the Kingdom.

God rewards the diligent—not just with money, but with influence, favor, and authority. Diligence is a divine principle that aligns your life with heavenly momentum. It turns your daily actions into a harvest that blesses not just you, but others. Just like a farmer doesn't reap unless he plows, plants, and waters, neither can we expect fruitfulness without consistent, faithful effort.

So here's the question: Are you showing up for what you're praying for? Are you stewarding your time, resources, and energy with diligence—or are you waiting for breakthrough while sitting in inactivity? The Law of Diligence may not be glamorous, but it is *guaranteed* to produce results.

Focus Point

"The soul of a lazy man desires, and has nothing; but the soul of the diligent shall be made rich." (Proverbs 13:4, NKJV)

This verse cuts to the heart of the matter. Desire alone is not enough. Many people want success, freedom, and financial breakthrough—but they're unwilling to embrace the daily discipline that makes it happen. God has tied prosperity to diligence—not to dreaming, not to wishing, but to faithful action over time.

Main Theme

The Law of Diligence is about spiritual and practical perseverance. It is the steady application of wisdom, effort, and faith over time. Diligence is what turns vision into reality, prayers into plans, and ideas into income. This chapter emphasizes that diligence is a lifestyle, not a season. It's what separates those who talk about change from those who actually walk into transformation. God honors the diligent because diligence reflects trust, maturity, and Kingdom stewardship.

"Breakthrough doesn't come to the busy—it comes to the diligent."

Key Scriptures

- *"The plans of the diligent lead surely to plenty, but those of everyone who is hasty, surely to poverty."* (Proverbs 21:5, NKJV)
- *"Do you see a man who excels in his work? He will stand before kings; he will not stand before unknown men."* (Proverbs 22:29, NKJV)
- *"He who has a slack hand becomes poor, but the hand of the diligent makes rich."* (Proverbs 10:4, NKJV)

Key Points

- **Diligence Is Consistent, Not Occasional** It's not what you do once in a while that changes your life—it's what you do consistently, day after day.
- **Desire Without Diligence Is Futile** Wishing without working leads to disappointment. Diligence transforms desire into destiny.
- **God Blesses Faithful Stewards** The Lord entrusts more to those who manage well what they already have. Diligence is proof you're ready for more.
- **Diligence Is Not Busyness** Being busy isn't the same as being fruitful. Diligence is focused, purpose-driven effort—not frantic activity.
- **The Diligent Stand Before Kings** Excellence attracts opportunity. When you do your work with care and intention, doors open that only diligence can unlock.
- **Diligence Builds Wealth Over Time** There are no overnight harvests in the Kingdom. But steady planting, watering, and labor will produce fruit in due season.
- **Diligence Is a Weapon Against Poverty** Scripture connects laziness to lack. Diligence is a divine strategy for escaping the cycle of lack and stepping into provision.

Journaling Questions

This chapter challenges you to examine how you're showing up each day. Through journaling, you'll evaluate whether your habits reflect your hopes and if your actions align with your prayers. The Law of Diligence invites you to shift from occasional inspiration to daily discipline.

As you reflect, you'll see where procrastination or passivity may be robbing you of increase. You'll begin to identify where your diligence needs to grow—whether in managing finances, developing a business, or pursuing spiritual maturity. The Holy Spirit will use this time to help you develop a diligence plan that honors God and leads to fruitfulness.

My Daily Investment

Do my daily actions reflect the future I say I want?

_____
_____
_____
_____
_____
_____
_____

Fruit vs. Frustration

Where in my life do I feel stuck—and could a lack of diligence be the reason?

_____
_____
_____
_____
_____
_____
_____

Faithfulness in the Small

Am I being diligent with what I currently have, or am I waiting for more before I act?

_____
_____
_____
_____
_____
_____
_____

Busyness or Diligence?

How can I distinguish between being busy and being genuinely productive?

_____
_____
_____
_____
_____
_____
_____

The Diligence Plan

What area of my life needs a new plan of consistent, focused diligence starting today?

_____
_____
_____
_____
_____
_____
_____

Actionable Steps

Cultivate Daily Faithfulness
Choose one area—spiritual (prayer, Bible study), financial (budgeting, saving), or physical (health, discipline)—and commit to 15 minutes a day for the next 21 days.

Equip Yourself with Tools for Consistency
Download an app, create a checklist, or set a recurring calendar reminder to keep you accountable. Diligence is easier when systems support it.

Engage a Diligence Partner
Find a friend, spouse, or mentor who can check in with you weekly about one area you're working on. Accountability fuels follow-through.

Personal Reflection

There's no mystery to the Law of Diligence—it's clear, it's consistent, and it's powerful. As you examine your life, ask yourself if your effort reflects your expectations. What you're praying for must also be what you're preparing for. God is not looking for perfect people—He's looking for faithful ones.

Diligence is more than hard work—it's holy work. It's how you turn your calling into impact. The world is full of distractions, but diligence keeps your eyes on the goal. As you continue growing, remember that excellence and breakthrough are the harvest of steady obedience.

What am I doing with the time God has given me? Where has diligence been lacking in my life? And am I ready to commit fully to the path that leads to fruitfulness?

_____
_____
_____
_____
_____
_____
_____
_____
_____
_____
_____
_____
_____
_____
_____
_____
_____
_____
_____
_____

Closing Prayer: *Lord, thank You for calling me to a life of diligence. Help me not to grow weary in doing good, but to be faithful in every season. Teach me to work with excellence, to manage my time with wisdom, and to pursue my calling with consistency. I choose to honor You today with diligent hands and a focused heart. In Jesus' name, Amen.*

Chapter 11

The Law of Risk

"But without faith it is impossible to please Him, for he who comes to God must believe that He is, and that He is a rewarder of those who diligently seek Him." (Hebrews 11:6, NKJV)

There was a time in my life when I stood on the edge of a major decision—one that felt risky, uncertain, and downright uncomfortable. I remember pacing the floor, asking God if I should step into a business venture that had the potential to change everything. It wasn't a reckless move. I had done my research. I had prayed. But still, the outcome wasn't guaranteed. And in that moment, I realized something profound: *faith always involves risk.*

Many people want success without uncertainty. They want results without the discomfort of risk. But the Kingdom doesn't operate that way. The parable of the talents makes it clear—those who played it safe were rebuked. It was the one who took what he was given and *did something with it* who was praised and promoted. God is not glorified by caution born out of fear—He's glorified by trust that acts even when the outcome isn't fully visible.

The Law of Risk challenges us to move beyond comfort and into calling. It asks, "What would you do if you weren't afraid?" Risk is not the enemy—it's the environment of faith. Every breakthrough in my life has come on the other side of a risk. Not a foolish gamble, but a calculated, prayerful, faith-filled step forward. Risk is how we partner with God to expand His Kingdom and our capacity.

So let me ask you: Are you burying your talent in the ground of fear? Or are you willing to step out, risk something meaningful, and believe that God is big enough to catch you if you fall—or elevate you if you fly?

Focus Point

"But without faith it is impossible to please Him..." (Hebrews 11:6, NKJV)

This verse reminds us that faith is more than belief—it's action. True faith requires movement, and movement requires risk. If everything in your life is certain, controlled, and comfortable, you may be missing the opportunity to truly please God. He delights in those who trust Him enough to take bold steps into the unknown.

Main Theme

The Law of Risk teaches that Kingdom wealth and impact are impossible without action rooted in faith. Playing it safe may feel secure, but it stifles potential and dishonors the opportunities God provides. Risk is the currency of faith. This chapter reveals that the greatest breakthroughs often come through uncomfortable decisions, uncertain steps, and calculated faith-based action. It's not about reckless leaps—it's about Spirit-led risks that stretch your faith and grow your influence.

> **"Your calling is always on the other side of your comfort zone."**

Key Scriptures

- *"To one he gave five talents, to another two, and to another one... But he who had received one went and dug in the ground, and hid his lord's money."* (Matthew 25:15, 18, NKJV)
- *"Cast your bread upon the waters, for you will find it after many days."* (Ecclesiastes 11:1, NKJV)
- *"For we walk by faith, not by sight."* (2 Corinthians 5:7, NKJV)

Key Points

- **Risk Is the Language of Faith** Faith isn't proven in feelings—it's revealed through movement. Every act of risk, when Spirit-led, is a statement of trust.

- **Playing It Safe Can Be Disobedience** The servant who buried his talent wasn't just cautious—he was unfaithful. Playing it safe can sometimes be a lack of obedience, not a sign of wisdom.
- **God Uses Risk to Grow You** Stepping into uncertainty stretches your capacity, sharpens your discernment, and strengthens your spiritual muscles.
- **Risk Requires Preparation and Prayer** God doesn't call you to jump blindly, but to plan wisely. When risk is birthed in prayer and prepared through strategy, it bears fruit.
- **Risk Often Precedes Promotion** Every new level requires a new leap. Don't wait until you feel fully ready—obedience often comes before full understanding.
- **The Cost of Inaction Is Higher Than You Think** Not taking a risk may feel like you're protecting yourself, but you may actually be forfeiting increase, growth, and Kingdom impact.
- **Obedient Risk Attracts God's Favor** When you step out in faith, heaven responds. God rewards those who believe enough to move, even when the destination isn't fully mapped out.

Journaling Questions

This chapter invites you to examine the risks you've taken—or avoided. Journaling through the Law of Risk will uncover fears, excuses, and hesitations that may be holding you back. It will also help you clarify which areas God may be calling you to trust Him more boldly.

You'll come to understand the difference between reckless decisions and faith-filled obedience. You'll uncover places where comfort has become your idol and where God is nudging you toward growth. This reflection will empower you to say yes to the hard things that lead to harvest.

Comfort vs. Calling

Where have I chosen comfort over the calling to step out in faith?

_____
_____
_____
_____
_____
_____
_____

Obedient Action

Is there a risk God has been asking me to take—but I've delayed out of fear?

_____
_____
_____
_____
_____

My Talent in the Ground

What resource, idea, or opportunity have I buried because I was afraid of failure?

_____
_____
_____
_____
_____
_____

Counting the Real Cost

What might I be losing by refusing to take a Spirit-led risk?

_____
_____
_____
_____
_____
_____

Faith in Motion

What's one bold step I can take this week to align with God's invitation into the unknown?

_____
_____
_____
_____
_____
_____

Actionable Steps

Cultivate a Risk-Taking Mindset
Begin a list called "If I wasn't afraid, I would..." Write down at least five things. Then pray over them and highlight one to pursue with God.

Equip with Wise Counsel
Find someone who has taken a similar risk and learn from them. Risk is easier when you learn from those who've walked the road ahead of you.

Engage the First Step
Choose one action this week that represents movement. Make the call, send the email, start the outline—do something that makes the risk real.

Personal Reflection

God didn't create you to live a life of fear-filled control. He designed you for boldness, faith, and movement. If you want to live a life that makes a difference, you'll have to step into places that feel uncertain. Risk isn't your enemy—it's your proving ground.

As you reflect on this chapter, remember that Jesus never called anyone to safety. He called them to purpose. The water didn't hold Peter up—the word of Jesus did. And the same word is calling you now: "Come." It's your turn to step out.

Where have I been playing it safe? What could obedience look like if I trusted God completely? And what risk am I being called to take that might change everything?

Closing Prayer: *Father, thank You for calling me beyond my comfort zone. Help me to trust You more than I trust certainty. Give me boldness to step out in faith, even when the outcome is unclear. I surrender fear and control. Teach me to take Spirit-led risks that honor You and expand Your Kingdom. In Jesus' name, Amen.*

CHAPTER 12

THE LAW OF LEVERAGE AND ACCELERATION

"One man of you shall chase a thousand, for the Lord your God is He who fights for you, as He promised you." (Joshua 23:10, NKJV)

I remember a moment in my journey when I realized I was doing *all* the work. I was putting in the hours, hustling every day, and getting results—but not the kind of multiplication I knew God had called me to walk in. That was the season I learned about leverage. It wasn't about doing *more* with my time; it was about using what I had—relationships, resources, systems, and ideas—in a way that produced greater impact with less effort. When I discovered leverage, I didn't just experience increase—I experienced *acceleration*.

Leverage is a Kingdom principle. God never meant for you to carry everything on your own. Just like Jesus multiplied the loaves and fishes through the hands of the disciples, God uses your seed, effort, and wisdom to produce *more* than you could ever generate by yourself. When we operate with leverage—using our finances, networks, time, and gifts wisely—God adds His super to our natural, creating exponential results.

Acceleration happens when we align our systems and stewardship with the power of God's timing. There are moments when you can sow and reap in the same season—not because you worked harder, but because you worked *smarter*, and with faith. Leverage turns effort into expansion. Acceleration turns obedience into overflow. Both require trust—and both are gifts God is ready to release when we steward wisely.

So I challenge you: Are you still trying to build with your own two hands what God wants to multiply through the tools and people around you? The Law of Leverage and Acceleration is not just about speed—it's about stewardship and supernatural partnership.

Focus Point

"One man of you shall chase a thousand..." (Joshua 23:10, NKJV)

This verse is a picture of supernatural leverage. It reminds us that, with God, one person can do the work of a thousand. Kingdom impact doesn't depend on your strength—it depends on your alignment. When you're in sync with God's strategy, your results are multiplied far beyond human capacity.

Main Theme

The Law of Leverage and Acceleration teaches us that God never intended for us to labor without increase. Instead, He's designed us to partner with Him and with others in ways that multiply our efforts. This law reveals how to use tools, systems, and relationships to maximize impact and unlock divine acceleration. Acceleration isn't the absence of process—it's the supernatural empowerment of it. Leverage uses what you already have. Acceleration moves you further, faster, when you walk in obedience and wisdom.

"Leverage multiplies your labor—acceleration multiplies your timeline."

Key Scriptures

- *"Two are better than one, because they have a good reward for their labor."* (Ecclesiastes 4:9, NKJV)
- *"Give, and it will be given to you: good measure, pressed down, shaken together, and running over..."* (Luke 6:38, NKJV)
- *"So is the kingdom of God, as if a man should scatter seed...and the earth yields crops by itself: first the blade, then the head..."* (Mark 4:26–28, NKJV)

Key Points

- **Leverage Is a Multiplier of Effort** With the right tools, relationships, or strategies, you can achieve more without working harder.

- **Acceleration Comes Through Alignment** When your timing aligns with God's will and systems are in place, you enter into seasons of rapid growth.
- **Stewardship Precedes Speed** God accelerates what is well-managed. Faithfulness prepares you for favor.
- **Partnership Is Divine Leverage** God brings people into your life who carry keys to your next level. Don't ignore the power of relational leverage.
- **Systems Create Speed** A good system works for you even when you're not present. Leverage includes automating what you once did manually.
- **Small Seeds, Big Harvests** The Kingdom operates on disproportionate return. What you sow in faith today can return in multiplied form tomorrow.
- **You're Not Supposed to Do It Alone** Acceleration happens when you stop trying to be a one-person show and start operating in the strength of shared vision.

Journaling Questions

This chapter helps you reflect on whether you're laboring or leveraging. It will challenge you to identify areas where you're limiting growth by relying solely on your own strength.

You'll begin to see what you're holding too tightly and where God wants to multiply your influence. You'll recognize the systems or relationships that are meant to speed your journey and invite the Holy Spirit to guide your next season with greater wisdom and flow.

My Multiplication Gaps

Where in my life am I still doing things manually that could be delegated, systematized, or supported?

_____
_____
_____
_____
_____
_____
_____

Relational Leverage

Who has God placed in my life to help carry this vision—and have I welcomed their help?

_____
_____
_____
_____
_____
_____

Spiritual Alignment

Have I been waiting for acceleration without aligning with God's strategy and timing?

_____
_____
_____
_____
_____
_____

Tool Check

What tools, platforms, or resources could I be using to multiply my effectiveness?

_____
_____
_____
_____
_____
_____

Acceleration Faith

Do I believe God can move me forward faster than human logic allows—and what step would reflect that faith?

_____
_____
_____
_____
_____
_____

Actionable Steps

Cultivate a Multiplier Mindset
List three areas of your life (business, ministry, finances, etc.) where you can replace effort with strategy or people. Choose one to restructure this week.

Equip with Scalable Tools
Pick one platform or tool (automation, scheduling, outsourcing, etc.) that can save you time and increase output. Implement it immediately.

Engage Strategic Partnerships
Identify one relationship you've underutilized and reach out this week with a clear invitation for collaboration or input.

Personal Reflection

Too often, we settle for survival when God is calling us to *scale*. As you reflect on the Law of Leverage and Acceleration, ask yourself whether you've been stuck in cycles of toil instead of entering rhythms of grace. What if your next breakthrough doesn't require more effort—but a wiser strategy?

God doesn't just want to add to your life—He wants to multiply it. But He requires stewardship, humility, and the willingness to shift how you operate. If you've been stuck, it may not be a lack of favor—it may be a lack of leverage.

What am I still trying to carry alone? What systems and people has God already provided for my growth? And what action can I take this week to shift from labor to leverage, and from striving to acceleration?

_____
_____
_____
_____
_____
_____
_____
_____
_____
_____
_____
_____
_____
_____
_____
_____
_____
_____
_____
_____
_____
_____
_____
_____
_____
_____
_____
_____
_____
_____

Closing Prayer: *Father, thank You for being the God of multiplication and acceleration. I surrender the areas where I've tried to build in my own strength. Show me how to work smarter, not just harder. Lead me to the people, tools, and systems that will multiply my purpose. I trust You for divine acceleration and receive the wisdom to steward it well. In Jesus' name, Amen.*

Chapter 13

The Law of Compounding

"For precept must be upon precept, precept upon precept, line upon line, line upon line, here a little, there a little." (Isaiah 28:10, NKJV)

There was a season in my life when I was investing faithfully—giving, saving, building, and stewarding my time and resources. But I didn't see immediate results. Days became weeks, weeks became months. I found myself asking, "Is this even working?" But then something began to shift. What started small started multiplying. It wasn't flashy, but it was steady. The results began compounding. And I realized—I had tapped into a divine principle: The Law of Compounding.

Compounding is more than a financial term. It's a Kingdom truth. God works through incremental obedience that builds momentum. Every act of faithfulness, every seed sown, every wise choice adds up. It may seem small in the moment, but over time it becomes powerful. The world often glorifies overnight success, but God honors consistent stewardship. The law of compounding reveals how growth happens when you refuse to quit.

Spiritually, emotionally, and financially, compounding works when you remain diligent over time. The Word of God compares spiritual maturity to building "line upon line." Wealth doesn't grow in spurts—it grows through consistent, strategic decisions. This law reminds us that the small things we do daily are creating the big outcomes we desire. Most people overestimate what they can do in a year and underestimate what they can do in ten.

So I'll ask you this: Are you honoring the process? Or are you jumping from one strategy to the next, hoping for quick results? The law of compounding invites you to trust the slow, steady, faithful path—and to believe that your consistency is building something that cannot be shaken.

Focus Point

"For precept must be upon precept, line upon line..." (Isaiah 28:10, NKJV)

This verse reveals the nature of God's process. Growth is not chaotic—it is ordered. It's structured. Just like brick upon brick builds a house, God builds wealth and character through steady layers of faithfulness. Compounding is the divine pattern of progress.

Main Theme

The Law of Compounding teaches that every wise decision made consistently over time leads to exponential growth. This applies to money, faith, relationships, and even influence. Nothing grows to fullness overnight. In the Kingdom, God blesses those who are faithful in little with much. Compounding is the divine result of faithful stewardship combined with the patience to see it through. Time is not your enemy—it's your greatest ally when you walk in wisdom.

"Consistency over time is the miracle God uses to multiply your life."

Key Scriptures

- *"He who is faithful in what is least is faithful also in much..."* (Luke 16:10, NKJV)
- *"Do not despise these small beginnings, for the Lord rejoices to see the work begin..."* (Zechariah 4:10, NLT)
- *"And let us not grow weary while doing good, for in due season we shall reap if we do not lose heart."* (Galatians 6:9, NKJV)

Key Points

- **Small Steps Lead to Big Impact** One right decision today can compound into tremendous fruit tomorrow. Never underestimate the power of small beginnings.

- **Time Is a Multiplier, Not a Thief** When stewarded well, time doesn't take away—it multiplies what you plant. Compounding is time working *for* you.
- **Faithfulness Fuels Growth** What you commit to consistently will eventually overflow. God honors sustained obedience.
- **Wealth Grows with Repetition** Financial growth isn't about one big break—it's about daily, wise habits that build over time.
- **Spiritual Growth Compounds Too** The more time you spend in prayer, the Word, and godly action, the more momentum your spiritual life gains.
- **Avoid the Trap of Impatience** Impatience aborts the power of compounding. Don't dig up what you've sown just because you don't see results yet.
- **The Greatest Rewards Come to Finishers** Long-term thinkers inherit long-term wealth. Stay the course—and watch what God does with your consistency.

Journaling Questions

This chapter invites you to evaluate your daily habits, long-term vision, and level of consistency. Journaling through the Law of Compounding will reveal how your small decisions are adding up—and where new patterns need to begin.

You'll gain clarity on what you're truly investing in—spiritually and financially—and whether your actions reflect your values. You'll also uncover opportunities to make small shifts that, over time, create major results.

My Compound Habits

What am I doing daily that will compound into the future I desire—or the one I want to avoid?

_____
_____
_____
_____
_____
_____

Faithfulness Check

Have I been consistent in the small things God has entrusted to me?

_____
_____
_____
_____
_____
_____

Patience in Progress

Where have I grown impatient, and how can I renew my trust in God's timing?

_____
_____
_____
_____
_____
_____

Strategic Sowing

What seeds am I planting now that I need to protect and water with diligence?

_____
_____
_____
_____
_____
_____

Long-Term Vision

What would change if I committed to a 10-year mindset rather than expecting overnight results?

_____
_____
_____
_____
_____
_____

Actionable Steps

Cultivate Consistency
Choose one habit—spiritually or financially—that you will commit to daily for the next 90 days. Don't skip. Don't stop.

Equip with Tracking Tools
Start a simple journal or app tracker to monitor progress. What gets tracked gets multiplied. Celebrate small milestones.

Engage in Long-Term Thinking
Write out a 3–5 year vision for your finances or spiritual walk. Review it weekly and ask: "What am I doing today that moves me closer to this?"

Personal Reflection

The most powerful changes in your life won't come through explosive events, but through consistent investment. As you reflect on this law, ask yourself: Am I planting the kind of seeds that will build the harvest I want to reap in 5, 10, or even 20 years?

God isn't asking for perfection. He's asking for persistence. The enemy loves to discourage you in the early stages—but God rejoices in every step forward. Your future is being built right now, one faithful act at a time.

What have I been building—line upon line? Have I honored the small beginnings? And what would my life look like if I stayed faithful long enough for compounding to do its full work?

Closing Prayer: *Father, thank You for the power of consistency. Help me to honor the process and not despise small beginnings. Teach me to invest my time, my energy, and my resources with wisdom and faith. I trust You for the harvest—even when I can't see it yet. Strengthen me to stay faithful. In Jesus' name, Amen.*

Chapter 14

The Law of Philanthrovesting

"Command those who are rich in this present age not to be haughty, nor to trust in uncertain riches but in the living God, who gives us richly all things to enjoy. Let them do good, that they be rich in good works, ready to give, willing to share." (1 Timothy 6:17–18, NKJV)

I remember the first time I realized that my financial decisions could ripple beyond my bank account and into eternity. It wasn't just about giving to a need—it was about *investing in a future that outlived me*. That realization didn't come in a moment of emotional generosity, but through a revelation of *purpose-driven wealth*. That's when the term philanthrovesting was born in my heart. It's not just about giving—it's about *sowing* where lives are transformed and legacies are built.

The Law of Philanthrovesting is where generosity and stewardship intersect. God never intended for us to amass wealth for comfort alone. We are called to be *channels*, not containers. True Kingdom wealth is measured not only by what you accumulate, but by what you release into the hands of God for His purposes. This is a higher level of financial thinking. It is giving with intentionality—strategic generosity with impact in mind.

When we adopt the mindset of a philanthrovestor, we stop giving based on emotion or guilt and start investing in vision, mission, and multiplication. This law transforms the way you look at money. Every dollar is a seed, and every seed carries potential to produce eternal fruit. It's not about how much you give—it's about how wisely and purposefully you give. When God finds someone He can trust with abundance, He routes it through them to reach others.

So I ask you: Are you a philanthropist or a philanthrovestor? Are you giving from obligation, or are you partnering with Heaven to fund the advancement of God's Kingdom on the earth? The harvest is waiting—but it takes intentional sowers to release it.

Focus Point

"Let them do good, that they be rich in good works, ready to give, willing to share." (1 Timothy 6:18, NKJV)

This verse doesn't condemn wealth—it redirects it. God richly gives us all things to enjoy, but commands us to be *rich in good works*. True wealth isn't found in what we hold—it's revealed in what we give. This is the heart of philanthrovesting: giving that builds people, purposes, and the Kingdom.

Main Theme

The Law of Philanthrovesting redefines the purpose of wealth. It's not merely about blessing the giver—it's about empowering the receiver and extending the reach of God's purposes. A philanthrovestor sees giving as a Kingdom investment strategy—intentional, prayerful, and strategic. This law teaches us to steward not just what we keep, but what we give away. It's how you plant now for a harvest that changes lives for generations.

> **"Your wealth is only as powerful as the vision you sow it into."**

Key Scriptures

- *"He who has pity on the poor lends to the Lord, and He will pay back what he has given."* (Proverbs 19:17, NKJV)
- *"Give, and it will be given to you: good measure, pressed down, shaken together, and running over..."* (Luke 6:38, NKJV)
- *"Honor the Lord with your possessions, and with the firstfruits of all your increase."* (Proverbs 3:9, NKJV)

Key Points

- **Giving Is a Strategic Investment** Philanthrovesting transforms your giving from random generosity into targeted Kingdom impact.
- **God Is Looking for Financial Funnels** When He finds someone who will release wealth with purpose, He entrusts them with more.
- **You're Funding Eternity, Not Just Charity** It's not about making donations—it's about building legacies that point people to Jesus.
- **Emotion Isn't a Strategy** While compassion is powerful, wise philanthrovestors give from prayer and vision, not just reaction.
- **Purpose-Driven Wealth Multiplies** Money aligned with God's heart always returns with increase—both seen and unseen.
- **Your Giving Can Solve Problems** Strategic generosity breaks cycles of poverty, funds missions, launches ministries, and creates change.
- **The Seed You Sow Outlives You** Philanthrovesting turns financial blessing into *spiritual inheritance*. It's giving that echoes in eternity.

Journaling Questions

This chapter invites you to reflect deeply on how and *why* you give. Journaling through the Law of Philanthrovesting will uncover your current patterns and invite you into a new way of viewing generosity as a calling—not just an action.

You'll see where your giving is already bearing fruit—and where it could be more strategic. You'll begin to pray differently about your finances, asking God to show you where your dollars will do the most for His Kingdom. You'll walk away with a renewed sense of purpose in every offering.

My Giving Mindset

Do I give from emotion, habit, or divine strategy—and what does that reveal about my heart?

_____
_____
_____
_____
_____
_____
_____

Seed Evaluation

Where has my giving produced fruit—and where has it lacked intentionality?

_____
_____
_____
_____
_____
_____
_____

Channel vs. Container

Am I acting more as a container of wealth, or a channel God can use for Kingdom purposes?

_____
_____
_____
_____
_____

Sowing with Vision

What causes, ministries, or people has God placed on my heart to begin sowing into more purposefully?

_____
_____
_____
_____
_____
_____

Living to Leave a Legacy

What would it look like to structure my giving to outlast my lifetime?

_____
_____
_____
_____
_____
_____

Actionable Steps

Cultivate a Philanthrovestor's Heart
Ask the Holy Spirit to show you three areas where your giving can become more strategic. Pray for clarity and vision in these areas.

Equip with a Giving Plan
Write out your personal Kingdom giving strategy. Set goals for generosity that include percentages, partners, and timing.

Engage with Purpose-Driven Partners
Research and connect with a ministry or cause that aligns with your calling. Begin sowing intentionally—financially, relationally, or through influence.

Personal Reflection

God didn't bless you just to bless you—He blessed you to bless others. As you reflect on this chapter, allow the Holy Spirit to stretch your understanding of giving. What if your money could preach a sermon long after you're gone? What if your generosity opened doors for someone else's destiny?

We are not here to build our own empires—we're here to advance the Kingdom. When you become a philanthrovestor, you enter into partnership with God in changing lives, communities, and generations. This is more than giving. It's sowing into eternal impact.

What does my giving reveal about my values? How can I make my generosity more strategic? And what kind of legacy do I want my wealth to build—one that fades or one that multiplies?

Closing Prayer: *Father, thank You for blessing me so that I can be a blessing. Teach me to give with wisdom and intentionality. Show me where to sow, and how to partner with You to change lives through my generosity. Let me be a faithful steward and a strategic giver—one who funds the future You are building. In Jesus' name, Amen.*

Chapter 15

The Law of Transformation

"And do not be conformed to this world, but be transformed by the renewing of your mind, that you may prove what is that good and acceptable and perfect will of God."
(Romans 12:2, NKJV)

I used to think transformation was a one-time spiritual event—something that happened when I first said yes to Jesus. But over time, I realized that transformation is a continual process, one that demands my mind, my motives, and my money align with God's purposes. The Law of Transformation isn't about cosmetic change—it's about core identity change. You don't just act differently; you *become* someone new.

God doesn't just want better behavior from you—He wants a renewed mind. He wants a heart set on His Kingdom, a mind that sees like He sees, and a life that reflects His glory. The Law of Transformation teaches us that real change starts inside and produces visible fruit outside. Transformation is Heaven's design for elevation, and it is how you break free from worldly limitation and step into supernatural potential.

———

Focus Point

"Be transformed by the renewing of your mind…" (Romans 12:2, NKJV)

This verse is an invitation to think differently, live differently, and believe differently. It reminds us that transformation isn't behavior modification—it's spiritual renovation. As your mind is renewed by the Word of God, your life begins to mirror Heaven's blueprint.

Main Theme

The Law of Transformation declares that sustainable change only happens through spiritual renewal. Conformity to the world leads to limitation. Transformation through God's Word leads to discernment, breakthrough, and destiny. This law is not about trying harder—it's about thinking higher. As you intentionally align your thoughts with God's truth, you unlock divine possibilities and gain clarity on God's perfect will for your life.

Key Scriptures

- "For as he thinks in his heart, so is he." *(Proverbs 23:7a, NKJV)*
- "Create in me a clean heart, O God, and renew a steadfast spirit within me." *(Psalm 51:10, NKJV)*
- "But we all, with unveiled face, beholding as in a mirror the glory of the Lord, are being transformed…" *(2 Corinthians 3:18, NKJV)*

Key Points

- **Transformation Starts Internally** External shifts are temporary without internal renewal. The Word of God must rewire your thinking.
- **Renewing the Mind is Daily Work** Transformation isn't a moment—it's a lifestyle of soaking in the truth and rejecting lies.
- **Spiritual Growth Requires Mental Shift** You can't walk in Kingdom success with a wilderness mindset. Old thoughts must be replaced.
- **Your Thoughts Shape Your Reality** As you think, you become. Renewing your mind opens doors to new levels of living.

- **God's Will is Unlocked through Transformation** A renewed mind allows you to recognize and align with God's good, acceptable, and perfect will.
- **Obedience Activates Change** It's not enough to know truth—you must act on it to see transformation take hold.
- **Transformation Breaks Limitation** Conforming keeps you small; transformation prepares you for influence and abundance.

Journaling Questions

This chapter calls you to assess where you are in your transformation journey. Are you merely behaving better, or are you truly becoming someone new in Christ? Reflect on your current thought patterns—are they rooted in truth or in culture, trauma, and tradition? Transformation demands a renewal of your entire internal operating system.

As you engage with this law, let the Word become your mirror. Replace toxic thoughts with Kingdom truths. And most importantly, don't just read—act. Real change is always proven in practice, not theory. Allow God to expand your identity, vision, and capacity through this ongoing process of transformation.

Mind Renewal

What thoughts or beliefs do I need to renew with God's Word today?

_____
_____
_____
_____

Internal Inventory

Are my decisions driven more by old patterns or by spiritual truth?

_____
_____
_____
_____
_____

OBEDIENCE CHECK

What has God asked me to do that I've resisted, and why?

_____
_____
_____
_____
_____
_____

SPIRITUAL CAPACITY

How is God stretching me to think, dream, and believe on a higher level?

_____
_____
_____
_____
_____
_____

BECOMING NEW

In what ways have I already seen transformation in my life, and where do I sense the next level is waiting?

_____
_____
_____
_____
_____
_____

Actionable Steps

Cultivate a Transformed Mindset
Identify one lie you've believed and replace it with three Scriptures that speak the truth. Declare these daily.

Equip Your Thought Life
Start a "Transformation Journal." Record verses, declarations, and reflections that reframe your thinking weekly.

Engage in Obedient Action
Ask the Holy Spirit for one step of obedience that aligns with the new identity He's cultivating in you—then act on it without delay.

Personal Reflection

God isn't after your performance—He's after your perspective. He wants you to think differently so you can live differently. Transformation is a sacred journey, and every thought surrendered to His truth is a brick laid on the road to destiny. What if the next breakthrough you need isn't in changing your circumstances, but in changing your mind?

_____
_____
_____
_____
_____
_____
_____
_____
_____
_____
_____
_____

Closing Prayer: *Father, I surrender my mind, my habits, and my ways of thinking to You. Transform me from the inside out. Help me see myself and my future through the lens of Your truth. Teach me to recognize what needs to be renewed and give me the courage to walk in obedience. Make me a reflection of Your glory through a life continually transformed. In Jesus' name, Amen.*

Chapter 16

The Law of the Triple Bottom Line

"Beloved, I pray that you may prosper in all things and be in health, just as your soul prospers."
(3 John 1:2, NKJV)

There was a time when I believed prosperity only referred to finances. But God's idea of success is holistic—He desires that we flourish in every area of life. The Law of the Triple Bottom Line opened my eyes to a new framework: God cares deeply about your faith, fruit, and finances. True prosperity is measured not just by what's in your wallet, but by what's in your soul and how you impact others.

When you embrace this law, you begin to live with divine alignment. You no longer chase success the world's way, but instead you steward every area of life—your spiritual walk, your purpose, and your resources—for Kingdom advancement. You are not blessed just to be blessed; you are blessed to be a blessing.

Focus Point

"Just as your soul prospers..." (3 John 1:2)

This phrase is the foundation of the triple bottom line. Prosperity isn't just financial—it's emotional, relational, and spiritual. God desires believers to live in balance, where soul health drives life outcomes.

Main Theme

The Law of the Triple Bottom Line redefines success by Kingdom standards. It affirms that God wants His people to prosper in faith (spiritual health), fruit (impact and productivity), and finances (material provision). When these three areas work together in harmony, you reflect Heaven's order in your earthly walk. This law challenges you to stop compartmentalizing and start integrating every area of life under God's authority.

Key Scriptures

- "The blessing of the Lord makes one rich, and He adds no sorrow with it." *(Proverbs 10:22, NKJV)*
- "You shall remember the Lord your God, for it is He who gives you power to get wealth..." *(Deuteronomy 8:18, NKJV)*
- "By this My Father is glorified, that you bear much fruit..." *(John 15:8, NKJV)*

Key Points

- **God Desires Wholeness, Not Just Wealth** Financial abundance means little without spiritual and emotional health.
- **Faith is Foundational** A prosperous soul anchors success. Without strong faith, other areas crumble.
- **Fruit Reflects Kingdom Impact** Your fruit—lives changed, purposes fulfilled—demonstrates spiritual maturity.
- **Finances Are Tools, Not Trophies** Money is meant to serve Kingdom purposes, not personal status.

- **The Triple Bottom Line is Interdependent** Each area—faith, fruit, and finances—supports the others. Neglecting one weakens all.
- **Stewardship, Not Ownership** Everything you manage—time, talents, and treasure—belongs to God.
- **Measure Success by God's Standards** Don't confuse busyness or money with fruitfulness.

Journaling Questions

Take time to evaluate your balance. Are you strong spiritually but lacking in productivity or financial stewardship? Or do you have fruit and finances but no soul rest? The Triple Bottom Line invites you to realign your life with God's full vision for prosperity. True success isn't having more—it's becoming whole.

Reflect on which area needs attention. Ask the Holy Spirit to highlight where growth is needed. Then pursue harmony by applying Kingdom principles in every part of your life. Wholeness is the goal, and God is the source.

Soul Check

Is my soul truly prospering, or am I spiritually dry beneath my productivity?

_____
_____
_____
_____

Faith Inventory

How does my daily schedule reflect my trust in God?

_____
_____
_____
_____
_____

Fruitfulness Evaluation

What impact am I having on others through my gifts and calling?

_____
_____
_____
_____
_____
_____

Financial Stewardship

Am I honoring God with how I manage money, or has money taken first place?

_____
_____
_____
_____
_____
_____

Triple Alignment

What's one small step I can take to bring my faith, fruit, and finances into better alignment?

_____
_____
_____
_____
_____
_____

Actionable Steps

Cultivate Wholeness
Start each day with a 10-minute check-in: How is my soul today? Use Scripture and prayer to guide your response.

Equip for Financial Wisdom
Take a practical step—such as creating a budget or giving consistently—to bring your finances under Kingdom principles.

Engage Your Fruitfulness
Identify one way your gifts can serve others this week. Use your fruit to bring someone closer to Christ or their purpose.

Personal Reflection

You were never meant to prosper in one area while lacking in others. God is not interested in fragmented success—He is a God of total restoration. The Triple Bottom Line reveals His heart for you: that you would flourish in faith, live purposefully, and steward abundance wisely. True prosperity is a three-stranded cord—and when it's in balance, your life becomes unshakable and impactful.

_____
_____
_____
_____
_____
_____
_____
_____
_____
_____
_____

Closing Prayer: Father, thank You for Your desire that I prosper in all things. Help me to align every part of my life with Your will—my faith, my fruit, and my finances. Where there is imbalance, bring order. Where there is lack, bring abundance. Where there is confusion, bring clarity. May I be a faithful steward of all You've given me, and may my life reflect Your Kingdom in fullness. In Jesus' name, Amen.

About the Author

Billy Epperhart is a successful entrepreneur, investor, and a nationally known speaker and author. He is the CEO of Andrew Wommack Ministries and Charis Bible College, as well as the cofounder of the Charis Business School. In addition, he oversees the strategic direction of his nonprofit, WealthBuilders, which provides financial and spiritual education to help people make sense of making money for making a difference. The missional arm of WealthBuilders, Tricord Global, provides microfinance loans and business training in developing nations.

Harrison House is a Spirit-filled, Word of Faith Christian publisher dedicated to spreading the message of faith, hope, and love through our wide range of inspiring publications. Committed to the messages that highlight the power of the Word and Spirit, we provide books, devotionals, and study guides that empower believers to live victorious, faith-filled lives.

Our resources are designed to help readers grow spiritually, strengthen their faith, and experience the transformative power of God's Word. Harrison House is passionate about equipping Christians with the tools they need to fulfill their divine purpose and impact the world for Christ.

www.ingramcontent.com/pod-product-compliance
Lightning Source LLC
Chambersburg PA
CBHW080738230426
43665CB00020B/2780